Michael M. Dediu

What is Life for Homo Sapiens post 2020?

Life is evolution by harmony,
not by natural selection for people

DERC Publishing House

Nashua, New Hampshire, U. S. A.

Published and printed in the
United States of America
On the Great Seal of the United States are included:
E Pluribus Unum (Out of many, one)
Annuit Coeptis (He has approved of the undertakings)
Novus Ordo Seclorum (New order of the ages)

Library of Congress Control Number: 2021909171

Dediu, Michael M.

What is Life for Homo Sapiens post 2020?
Life is evolution by harmony, not by natural selection for people

ISBN-13: 978-1-950999-38-5

MSG0638047_46VPr1MAS1fZ1S0tA73b
1-10473311901
1-4T7JF85
1-4T7JF8C
26S4UQD5

Preface

What is life? There are many fundamental questions that all human beings are called to answer. The most important philosophers, including Socrates, Plato, Aristotle, Descartes, and Kant, always asked profound questions, and gave eternal answers.

Over 160 years ago, in 1859, the 50 years old Charles Darwin (12 February 1809 – 19 April 1882, aged 73.1) formulated the theory of evolution by natural selection, first presented in his book "On the Origin of Species" - it is the process by which all species of organisms change over time as a result of changes in heritable physical or behavioral traits. This was erroneously applied to humans too, mostly in a very wrong way.

Also, Darwin said "To kill an error is as good a service as, and sometimes even better than, the establishing of a new truth or fact." This is what we are doing in this book - the theory of evolution by natural selection does not apply to Homo Sapiens post 2020 – now we have evolution by harmony!

This book discusses in detail this important change, using many questions, giving complete responses, emphasizing on the new ideas from the Constitution of the World, which will create the conditions for a peaceful, free, harmonious and prosperous new country, Peaceful Terra.

The future begins to take shape in front of our eyes, and it is astonishingly beautiful!

Michael M. Dediu, Ph. D.

Nashua, New Hampshire, U. S. A., 17 May 2021

USA, New York, on Fifth Avenue at E 40th St, looking southwest at Mid-Manhattan Library, a New York Public Library (1895, 1908, 87 branches (Carnegie libraries (Andrew Carnegie (1835-1919)))), 53 millions of books and other items, the 2nd largest public library in the United States (behind the Library of Congress), and the fourth largest in the world (after British Library (170 M), Library of Congress (160 M), and Library and Archives Canada (54 M)) image archive (left), having thousands of photos, posters, illustrations, and other images.

Table of Contents

Question 1. What is life and why evolution by harmony?

Response 1. Life is a very complex structure, which includes the cell, the gene, the evolution by harmony for humans after 2020, (evolution by natural selection for the rest), as well as chemistry, mathematics, information, art, music, etc.

The change to evolution by harmony for humans after 2020 is because people finally arrived at a level of evolution where the natural selection was replaced by harmony – the best proof is the new Constitution of the World, whose objective is simply to help all the people on Earth to live better, peacefully, free, healthy, harmoniously, and prosperous.

More precisely, the Constitution starts with 7 details about its objectives:

We, the People on this Earth, in order to
1.1 - completely eliminate war and any type of conflicts,
1.2 - have a peaceful and harmonious world,
1.3 - have freedom, dignity, good families and respect,
1.4 - have good health and good education,
1.5 - have a friendly atmosphere and prosperity,
1.6 – have the safety and wellbeing of all the people in the world as the highest priority,
1.7 – use the best peaceful results, experience and knowledge of all current countries,

establish this Constitution of the World.

UK, London, from Westminster Bridge Road looking west to the bridge with the railroads going to Waterloo Station (to right), and to new original buildings on Westminster Bridge Road at Lambeth Palace Road, south of the Park Plaza Westminster Bridge London Hotel (to right), 400 m east from the Westminster Bridge ((1862, 250 m, width 26 m, 7 spans), 600 m southeast from the London Eye (2000), and 500 m south from the Waterloo Station (1922, 24 platforms, railway terminus, and underground, in Lambeth).

Question 2. Is Darwinism dead in water, and what is the first priority?

Response 2. No, Darwinism is not dead, it is valid for all other species, but not anymore for people, who past the natural selection phase. Now peace is the first priority – without peace not much can be done. Actually, conflicts and war are a return to natural selection – the stronger enslaves or kills the weaker.

Italy, Venezia, Giardini Reali (left), Il Campanile from Piazza San Marco, Libreria Sansoviniana (center), and Palazzo Ducale (right).

USA, New York, on West 42nd Street at Fifth Avenue, looking southeast at Chrysler building (back up, Walter P. Chrysler (1875-1940), 1930, 319 m, 77 floors, 111,000 m^2 floor area, 32 elevators, at Lexington Avenue), before it is Grand Hyatt New York Hotel (1919, 90 m), and before it is Grand Central Terminal (1871, 1903, 1913, 2000, built by Cornelius Vanderbilt (1794-1877, the 2nd richest American, after John D. Rockefeller (1839-1937)) and his 13 children, commuter railroad terminal, with a grand façade and concourse, at Park Avenue, 47 acres, 44 high-level platforms, 67 tracks on 2 levels).

Question 3. How Did Darwin define evolution and how many countries should be on Earth?

Response 3. Darwin said that evolution is "descent with modification," and the method is natural selection - this is true, but not for humans now – all people want just one beautiful and harmonious country - Peaceful Terra.

All the people of the world will be proud citizens of only one country, called Peaceful Terra, with total area of over 509 M km^2, and land area over 148 M km^2.

Being just one country, there are no borders:

UK, London, Mansion House (1753, center, the official residence of the Lord Mayor of London, Palladian (Palladio (1508-1580) architecture

Question 4. How do biological entities communicate, and how many rules will be in this Peaceful Terra?

Response 4. This question - how do biological entities communicate, or create new structures, or measure, or decide, or look for food, in other words how they do all the things necessary for survival – can be answered using mathematics, for example partial differential equation modeling.

Regarding the rules - not too many:

All the rules – not more than 2,000, on maximum 1,000 pages - on our Earth will be established by the people and their elected Advisers.

All rules proposed by Advisers must be approved by their 5 assistants (doctors, mathematicians, CEOs, engineers and teachers), and for any new rule over 2,000 basic rules (each rule on at most half a page, total 1,000 pages), at least on old rule must be eliminated.

All the rules can be changed or eliminated when a majority of the people or their Advisors agree, but some fundamental peace and order rules will remain.

Question 5. Is social Darwinism dead, and how will this Peaceful Terra be administrated?

Response 5. Yes, social Darwinism – which is the false theory that human groups and races are under the same rules of natural selection as Charles Darwin supposed to be in plants and animals in nature – is dead.

Peaceful Terra, being a very big country, will be divided in 10 simple regions:

For easier administration, Peaceful Terra will be only administratively divided in 10 simple and friendly regions of around 770 M people each, called R0, R1,…, R9, which will be delimited by meridians (or line of longitudes), with the assistance of the United Nations.

Italy, Venezia, exiting from under the Ponte di Rialto, seen from north, with houses on the south bank of Canal Grande

Question 6. Is adaptation to an environment important, and where will the capital of this Peaceful Terra be?

Response 6. Yes, in general, organisms that are better adapted to an environment will survive and reproduce, but humans these days can modify the environment, and make it more friendly for them.

The capital can be everywhere! Because the capitals tend to become huge bureaucracies, with lots of people trying to be there, without much usefulness, Peaceful Terra will have moving capitals, to benefit everybody.

Each region will have a pair of capitals plus an outside city, for better and more homogenous management (all will change every year; more details are in the annex book "World with One Country & its Ten Friendly Regions - Moving from 195 disagreeing countries, to 1 country with 10 collaborating regions"). For example, the first implementation will be:

R0 between meridians 0 and 15^0 E, capitals: Bern (Switzerland), Libreville (Gabon), and Oxford (UK).

R1: 15^0 E - 30^0 E, Warsaw (Poland), Pretoria (South Africa) and Miami (FL, USA).

R2: 30^0 E - 45^0 E, Moscow (Russia), Cairo (Egypt), and Grenoble (France).

R3: 45^0 E - 75^0 E, Astana (Kazakhstan), Karachi (Pakistan), and Montpellier (France).

R4: 75^0 E - 85^0 E, New Delhi (India), Novosibirsk (Russia), and Magdeburg (Germany).

R5: 85^0 E - 100^0 E, Krasnoyarsk (Russia), Urumqi (China), and Avignon (France).

R6: 100^0 E - 115^0 E, Jakarta (Indonesia), Beijing (China), and Neuchâtel (Switzerland).

R7: 115^0 E - 180^0, Tokyo (Japan), Sydney (Australia), and Malmö (Sweden).

R8: 180^0 - 70^0 Washington (USA), Mexico City (Mexico), and Bellinzona (Switzerland).
R9: 70^0 W – 0 Halifax (Canada), Brasilia (Brazil), and Biel (Switzerland).

UK, London, Inside Liverpool Street Station (1874, serving the east of UK)

There are many big differences between the populations of different regions, in the first implementation, but this will easily be corrected.

In the first implementation presented in Proposition 3, there are many big differences between the populations of different regions, and then between the populations of different sub-regions, but this is just the first implementation, which needs to be quickly put in place, and then, very easily, the delimitations will be moved a few kilometers east or west, to reach a balanced population.

Because all the people are in the same country, it is normal to modify a little its regions, for better administration, to make everybody happy.

It is well understood that there will be some difficulties in the beginning, like in all beginnings, but with calm, patience, perseverance and hard work, the things will improve fast, and all the people will enjoy a better life.

Question 7. What are the main points of natural selection, and how many subdivisions will be in each Region?

Response 7. The main points of natural selection are variation, inheritance, selection, time and adaptation, but for humans the evolution is by harmony – those who are more harmonious with others will have a better evolution, and this will encourage others to be more harmonious.

Each of the 10 regions will be divided by meridians in 10 sub-regions S00,   , S99, each with about 77 M people.

Then each of the 100 sub-regions will be divided in 10 districts:

Each of the 100 sub-regions will be divided in 10 districts D000, D001,   , D999, each with about 7.7 M people, and each of the districts will have their current small and big cities.

All these delimitations between regions, as well as between sub-regions, will be flexible:

There will be just simple administrative delimitations, and all these delimitations between regions, as well as between sub-regions, will be flexible – they will be changed after each census (5 years), for maintaining a balanced number of people in all regions (around 770 M) and sub-regions (around 77 M).

Question 8. Are children important for the evolution by harmony, and why are the meridians used for divisions?

Response 8: Yes, children are very important, because those who are more harmonious will have more children – around three per family.

Meridians are easy to use, impartial, helpful for people with telework:

Having telework, many people will have a northern residence and a southern residence, seasonally moving from one to the other, to avoid extreme cold or heat, and having the same hour.

Italy, Venezia, Under the Ponte di Rialto, seen from north, with Fermata Rialto (center), and palazzi on the north bank of Canal Grande.

Question 9. What is the harmony role in the status of the oceans?

Response 9: Harmony is essential -all the oceans will belong to some of the regions, and working harmoniously to maintain and clean the oceans will give beautiful results:

All the oceans will belong to some of the regions defined above, therefore will be maintained by those regions, to be free of any piracy or other bad activity – World Police will help when necessary.

The harmony will generate strong cooperation for the maintenance of the oceans, which will also become residence for many people.

UK, London, from a double deck bus on the London Bridge, looking northeast to the Regis House (center left), and other buildings near Liverpool St.

Question 10. What Alfred Wallace did and how the World Government looks like?

Response 10: Alfred Wallace (1823 – 1913, 90) was a British naturalist, who co-developed the theory of natural selection and evolution with Charles Darwin, who was 14 years older; in 1859, when Darwin was 50 years old, Wallace was 36, in 1882, when Darwin died at 73, Wallace was 59, and lived 31 more years.

The family of over 7. 7 B people from Peaceful Terra will have four levels of world management; at the local level, if needed, it could be one or two more levels of local managers (mayors, town managers, county managers – all levels of management must be friendly, helpful, fast, polite, modest and smart):

Level 1 Management: 1,000 L1 friendly managers, for the 1,000 districts, who will supervise and assist the mayors and town managers from their district, for a total of about 7,700,000 people in each district. Each of the 1,000 L1 friendly managers will be located in a central city from their districts – they could be the mayors of those cities, but with new responsibilities for the whole district.

Level 2 Management: 100 L2 friendly managers, for the 100 sub-regions, who will supervise and assist the 10 L1 managers of the 10 districts of each sub-region, for a total of about 77,000,000 people for each sub-region. These 100 L2 friendly managers will move each month between the two capitals of each of the 100 sub-regions.

USA< New York, on 7th Avenue at West 57th Street, looking southwest: right: a classical building, which is tangent to the right, on W 57th St, to the American Fine Arts Society building (1892); left down: a beautiful building, opposite Carnegie Hall (to the left, across 7th Ave, 1891, concert hall with exceptional acoustics, architecture and performance history); left up: an impressive double skyscraper, with the southwest side on W 56th St.

Question 11. How does harmony help to choose the two capitals for each sub-region?

Response 11: Discussing with people in a harmonious atmosphere and understanding each other, will certainly help to choose, in the beginning, these capitals:

In Region R0: from Paris (France) to N'Djamena (Chad)

- The sub-region R00 will have the capitals Paris (France) and Niamey (Niger) – assistance from Magdeburg (Germany).
- The sub-region R01 will have the capitals Brussels (Belgium) and Porto-Novo (Benin) - assistance from Toronto (Canada).
- The sub-region R02 will have the capitals Amsterdam (Netherlands) and Algiers (Algeria) - assistance from Graz (Austria).
- The sub-region R03 will have the capitals Luxembourg (Luxembourg) and Sao Tome (Sao Tome and Principe) - assistance from Adelaide (Australia).
- The sub-region R04 will have the capitals of Abuja (Nigeria) and Bochum (Germany) - assistance from Nikko (Japan).
- The sub-region R05 will have the capitals Malabo (Equatorial Guinea), and Zürich (Switzerland) - assistance from Leeds (UK).
- The sub-region R06 will have the capitals Oslo (Norway) and Tunis (Tunisia) - assistance from Sheffield (UK).
- The sub-region R07 will have the capitals Roma (Italy) and Luanda (Angola) - assistance from Yamagata (Japan).
- The sub-region R08 will have the capitals in Berlin (Germany) and Tripoli (Libya) - assistance from New York (USA).
- The sub-region R09 will have the capitals Prague (Czech Republic) and N'Djamena (Chad) - assistance from Brisbane (Australia).

UK, London, from a double deck bus on the London Bridge, looking to the east at the Tower Bridge, HMS Belfast (center left on Thames

In Region R1: from Zagreb (Croatia) to Bujumbura (Burundi)

- The sub-region R10 will have the capitals in Zagreb (Croatia) and Brazzaville (Congo) - assistance from Nantes (France).
- The sub-region R11 will have the capitals in Vienna (Austria), Windhoek (Namibia) - assistance from Bilbao (Spain).
- The sub-region R12 will have the capitals in Stockholm (Sweden), Bangui (Central African Republic) - assistance from Florence (Italy).
- The sub-region R13 will have the capitals in Budapest (Hungary), Rundu (Namibia) - assistance from Monaco (Monaco).
- The sub-region R14 will have the capitals in Belgrade (Serbia), Kananga (Democratic Republic of Congo) - assistance from Liverpool (UK).
- The sub-region R15 will have the capitals in Athens (Greece), Mongu (Zambia) - assistance from Los Angeles (CA, USA).
- The sub-region R16 will have the capitals in Helsinki (Finland) and Kolwezi (Democratic Republic of the Congo) - assistance from Montreal (Canada).
- The sub-region R17 will have the capitals in Bucharest (Romania) and Gaborone (Botswana) - assistance from Philadelphia (PA, USA).
- The sub-region R18 will have the capitals in Minsk (Belarus) and Maseru (Lesotho) - assistance from Orleans (France).
- The sub-region R19 will have the capitals in Chisinau (Republic of Moldova) and Bujumbura (Burundi) - assistance from Hamburg (Germany).

USA, New York, at 745 7th Avenue at W 50th St, looking south, Barclays Corporate Office (British multinational banking & financial services).

In Region R2: from Kiev (Ukraine) to Baghdad (Iraq)

- The sub-region R20 will have the capitals in Kiev (Ukraine) and Kigali (Rwanda) - assistance from Ottawa (Canada).
- The sub-region R21 will have the capitals in Ankara (Turkey) and Khartoum (Sudan) - assistance from Salzburg (Austria).
- The sub-region R22 will have the capitals in Lilongwe (Malawi) and Nicosia (Cyprus) - assistance from Dallas (TX, USA).
- The sub-region R23 will have the capitals in Jerusalem (Israel) and Dodoma (Tanzania) - assistance from Strasbourg (France).
- The sub-region R24 will have the capitals in Damascus (Syria) and Nairobi (Kenya) - assistance from Stuttgart (Germany).
- The sub-region R25 will have the capitals in Krasnodar (Russia) and Addis Ababa (Ethiopia) - assistance from Marseille (France).
- The sub-region R26 will have the capitals in Rostov-on-Don (Russia) and Asmara (Eritrea) - assistance from Leipzig (Germany).
- The sub-region R27 will have the capitals in Stavropol (Russia) and Djibouti (Djibouti) - assistance from Zürich (Switzerland).
- The sub-region R28 will have the capitals in Mosul (Iraq) and Moroni (Comoros) - assistance from Linz (Austria).
- The sub-region R29 will have the capitals in Yerevan (Armenia) and Baghdad (Iraq) - assistance from Göttingen (Germany).

UK, London, from a double deck bus on Borough High St, looking northeast at The Shard (306 m, glass and steel).

In Region R3: from Riyadh (Saudi Arabia) to Malé (Maldives)

- The sub-region R30 will have the capitals in Riyadh (Saudi Arabia) and Mogadishu (Somalia) - assistance from Bonn (Germany).
- The sub-region R31 will have the capitals in Baku (Azerbaijan) and Antananarivo (Madagascar) - assistance from Le Mans (France).
- The sub-region R32 will have the capitals in Oral (Kazakhstan) and Tehran (Iran) - assistance from Pisa (Italy).
- The sub-region R33 will have the capitals in Ashgabat (Turkmenistan) and Abu Dhabi (United Arab Emirates) - assistance from Wolfsburg (Germany).
- The sub-region R34 will have the capitals in Magnitogorsk (Russia) and Muscat (Oman) - assistance from Toulouse (France).
- The sub-region R35 will have the capitals in Chelyabinsk (Russia) and Herat (Afghanistan) - assistance from Basel (Switzerland).
- The sub-region R36 will have the capitals in Tyumen (Russia) and Kandahar (Afghanistan) - assistance from Nagoya (Japan).
- The sub-region R37 will have the capitals in Dushanbe (Tajikistan) and Labytnangi (Russia) - assistance from Limoges (France).
- The sub-region R38 will have the capitals in Tashkent (Uzbekistan) and Kabul (Afghanistan) - assistance from Rostock (Germany).
- The sub-region R39 will have the capitals in Islamabad (Pakistan) and Malé (Maldives) - assistance from La Rochelle (France).

USA, Cape Cod, on the MacMillan Pier (600 m southeast from Pilgrim Monument (back center), Provincetown)

In Region R4: from Bishkek (Kyrgyzstan) to Brahmapur (India)

- The sub-region R40 will have the capitals in Bishkek (Kyrgyzstan) and Jaipur (India) - assistance from Osaka (Japan).
- The sub-region R41 will have the capitals in Akola (India) and Kashgar (China) - assistance from Genoa (Italy).
- The sub-region R42 will have the capitals in Almaty (Kazakhstan) and Coimbatore (India) - assistance from Perth (Australia).
- The sub-region R43 will have the capitals in Kuybyshev (Russia) and Agra (India) - assistance from Fukuoka (Japan).
- The sub-region R44 will have the capitals in Vertikos (Russia) and Nagpur (India) - assistance from Coral Bay (Australia).
- The sub-region R45 will have the capitals in Chennai (India) and Colombo (Sri Lanka) - assistance from Sapporo (Japan).
- The sub-region R46 will have the capitals in Lucknow (India) and Fedosikha (Russia) - assistance from Niigata (Japan).
- The sub-region R47 will have the capitals in Bilaspur (India) and Kolpashevo (Russia) - assistance from Albany (Australia).
- The sub-region R48 will have the capitals in Visakhapatnam (India) and Barnaul (Russia) - assistance from Hiroshima (Japan).
- The sub-region R49 will have the capitals in Brahmapur (India) and Tomsk (Russia) - assistance from Yokohama (Japan).

In Region R5: from Kathmandu (Nepal) to Dehong (China)

- The sub-region R50 will have the capitals in Kathmandu (Nepal) and Patna (India) - assistance from Kobe (Japan).
- The sub-region R51 will have the capitals in Bayingol (China) and Novokuznetsk (Russia) - assistance from Vichy (France).
- The sub-region R52 will have the capitals in Thimphu (Bhutan) and Dhaka (Bangladesh) - assistance from Jena (Germany).
- The sub-region R53 will have the capitals in Lhasa (China) and Achinsk (Russia) - assistance from Reims (France).
- The sub-region R54 will have the capitals in Abakan (Russia) and Kumul (China) - assistance from Fribourg (Switzerland).
- The sub-region R55 will have the capitals in Kyzyl (Russia) and Dibrugarh (India) - assistance from Denmark (Australia).
- The sub-region R56 will have the capitals in Bassein (Myanmar) and Tinsukia (India) - assistance from Chiba (Japan).
- The sub-region R57 will have the capitals in Yushu City (China) and Tinskoy (Russia) - assistance from Klagenfurt (Austria).
- The sub-region R58 will have the capitals in Jiuquan (China) and Medan (Indonesia) - assistance from Lucerne (Switzerland).
- The sub-region R59 will have the capitals in Chiang Mai (Thailand) and Dehong (China) - assistance from Mulhouse (France).

UK, London, from a cabin (moving down) on the London Eye, looking north at other cabins, loading and unloading area (center right), over Thames (left and down), with the London Eye pier (center left).

In Region R6: from Bangkok (Thailand) to Chita (Russia)

- The sub-region R60 will have the capitals in Bangkok (Thailand) and Kuala Lumpur (Malaysia) - assistance from Besançon (France).
- The sub-region R61 will have the capitals in Vientiane (Laos) and Singapore – assistance from Freiburg im Breisgau (Germany).
- The sub-region R62 will have the capitals in Phnom Penh (Cambodia) and Irkutsk (Russia) – assistance from Baden (Switzerland).
- The sub-region R63 will have the capitals in Palembang (Indonesia), Hanoi (Vietnam) – assistance from Thun (Switzerland).
- The sub-region R64 will have the capitals in Ulan Bator (Mongolia) and Ulan-Ude (Russia) – assistance from Chaumont (France).
- The sub-region R65 will have the capitals in Cirebon (Indonesia) and Nanning (China) – assistance from Vaduz (Lichtenstein).
- The sub-region R66 will have the capitals in Pontianak (Indonesia) and Baotou (China) – assistance from Lugano (Switzerland).
- The sub-region R67 will have the capitals in Surakarta (Indonesia) and Yichang (China) – assistance from Thonon-les-Bain (France).
- The sub-region R68 will have the capitals in Surabaya (Indonesia) and Changsha (China) – assistance from Burgdorf (Switzerland).
- The sub-region R69 will have the capitals in Chita (Russia) and Hong Kong (China) – assistance from Colmar (France).

Italy, Venezia, Ponte di Rialto (1588 – 1591) with Fermata Rialto (right), seen from south.

In Region R7: from Nanchang (China) to Melbourne (Australia)

- The sub-region R70 will have the capitals in Bandar Seri Begawan (Brunei Darussalam) and Nanchang (China) – assistance from Turku (Finland).
- The sub-region R71 will have the capitals in Krasnokamensk (Russia) and Jinan (China) – assistance from St. Gallen (Switzerland).
- The sub-region R72 will have the capitals in Baguio City (Philippines) and Hangzhou (China) – assistance from Dole (France).
- The sub-region R73 will have the capitals in Manila (Philippines) and Taipei (Taiwan, China) – assistance from Metz (France).
- The sub-region R74 will have the capitals in Kupang (Indonesia) and Shanghai (China) – assistance from Davos (Switzerland).
- The sub-region R75 will have the capitals in Pyongyang (North Korea) and Seoul (South Korea) – assistance from Versailles (France).
- The sub-region R76 will have the capitals in Vladivostok (Russia) and Busan (South Korea) – assistance from Innsbruck (Austria).
- The sub-region R77 will have the capitals in Kyoto (Japan) and Khabarovsk (Russia) – assistance from Germering (Germany).
- The sub-region R78 will have the capitals in Nagoya (Japan) and Komsomolsk-on-Amur (Russia) – assistance from Venice (Italy).
- The sub-region R79 will have the capitals in Sendai (Japan) and Melbourne (Australia) – assistance from St. Moritz (Switzerland).

UK, London, from a capsule of the London Eye, looking southwest at Big Ben (right up), Westminster Bridge, Westminster Palace (center up).

In Region R8: from Anchorage (Alaska, USA) to Lima (Peru)

- The sub-region R80 will have the capitals in Uelen (Russia) and Anchorage (Alaska, USA), – assistance from Zug (Switzerland).
- The sub-region R81 will have the capitals in Vancouver (Canada) and San Jose (CA, USA) – assistance from Odense (Denmark).
- The sub-region R82 will have the capitals in Vernon (Canada) and Los Angeles (CA, USA) – assistance from Amstetten (Austria).
- The sub-region R83 will have the capitals in Calgary (Canada) and Tijuana (Mexico) – assistance from Chur (Switzerland).
- The sub-region R84 will have the capitals in Hermosillo (Mexico) and Tucson (AR, USA) – assistance from Bergen (Norway).
- The sub-region R85 will have the capitals in Chihuahua (Mexico) and Regina (Canada) – assistance from Gothenburg (Sweden).
- The sub-region R86 will have the capitals in San Luis Potosi City (Mexico) and Winnipeg (Canada) – assistance from Yverdon-les-Bains (Switzerland).
- The sub-region R87 will have the capitals in Tulsa (OK, USA) and Veracruz (Mexico) – assistance from Bregenz (Austria).
- The sub-region R88 will have the capitals in Memphis (TN, USA) and San José (Costa Rica) – assistance from Uppsala (Sweden).
- The sub-region R89 will have the capitals in Lima (Peru) and Boston (MA, USA) – assistance from Tampere (Finland).

USA, Bretton Woods, the fire pit and the northeast part of the Mount Washington Resort (1902, elevation 500 m).

In Region R9: from La Paz (Bolivia) to London (United Kingdom)

- The sub-region R90 will have the capitals in La Paz (Bolivia) and Bangor (Maine, USA) – assistance from Aosta (Italy).
- The sub-region R91 will have the capitals in Caracas (Venezuela) and Road Town (British Virgin Islands) – assistance from Obergoms (Switzerland).
- The sub-region R92 will have the capitals in Buenos Aires (Argentina) and Fort-de-France (Martinique) – assistance from Freudenstadt (Germany).
- The sub-region R93 will have the capitals in Asuncion (Paraguay) and Montevideo (Uruguay) – assistance from Winterthur (Switzerland).
- The sub-region R94 will have the capitals in Cayenne (French Guiana), St. John's (Canada) – assistance from Novara (Italy).
- The sub-region R95 will have the capitals in Rio de Janeiro (Brazil) and Dakar (Senegal) – assistance from Toyama (Japan).
- The sub-region R96 will have the capitals in Freetown (Sierra Leone) and Lisbon (Portugal) – assistance from Kawasaki (Japan).
- The sub-region R97 will have the capitals in Bamako (Mali) and Athlone (Ireland) – assistance from Ulm (Germany).
- The sub-region R98 will have the capitals in Yamoussoukro (Cote d'Ivoire) and Madrid (Spain) – assistance from Okayama (Japan).
- The sub-region R99 will have the capitals in Ouagadougou (Burkina Faso) and London (United Kingdom) - assistance from Vaasa (Finland).

Italy, Venezia, Palazzi Contarini Fasan (left), Tiepolo (center-right) and Treves de Bonfili (right), north bank, 350 m west of Piazza San Marco

Question 12. How is harmony helping when disagreement appears at the Level 3 Management?

Response 12: The ten Level 3 friendly managers for the 10 regions will have plenty of disagreements, but they will harmoniously work, using calm and convincing arguments, to clarify the issues, and return to harmonious working environment.

Level 3 Management: Ten L3 friendly managers for the 10 regions, who will supervise and assist the 10 L2 managers of the 10 sub-regions of each region, for a total of about 770,000,000 people for each region.

- The Region R0 will have the first capitals in

Bern (Switzerland) and Libreville (Gabon) – assistance from Oxford (UK).

For better quality and consistency of the management, we'll have the first two cities from the region R0, and the third city from outside. Actually, being inside the same country Terra, any city, sub-region or region can ask for advice or help from anybody.

- The Region R1 will have the first capitals in

Warsaw (Poland) and Pretoria (South Africa) – assistance from Miami (FL, USA).

- The Region R2 will have the first capitals in

Moscow (Russia) and Cairo (Egypt) – assistance from Grenoble (France).

- The Region R3 will have the first capitals in

Astana (Kazakhstan) and Karachi (Pakistan), – assistance from Montpellier (France).

UK, London, inside Waterloo train station (1922, left side, UK's largest), with Waterloo Underground Station entrance (center right back).

- The Region R4 will have the first capitals in

New Delhi (India) and Novosibirsk (Russia) – assistance from Magdeburg (Germany).

- The Region R5 will have the first capitals in

Krasnoyarsk (Russia) and Urumqi (China) – assistance from Avignon (France).

- The Region R6 will have the first capitals in

Jakarta (Indonesia) and Beijing (China) – assistance from Neuchâtel (Switzerland).

- The Region R7 will have the first capitals in

Tokyo (Japan) and Sydney (Australia) – assistance from Malmö (Sweden).

- The Region R8 will have the first capitals in

Washington (USA) and Mexico City (Mexico) – assistance from Bellinzona (Switzerland).

- The Region R9 will have the first capitals in

Halifax (Canada) and Brasilia (Brazil) – assistance from Biel (Switzerland).

UK, London, from an ovoidal capsule of the London Eye, looking northeast at the two supporting arms. The London Eye - a giant Ferris wheel on the South (right) Bank of the River Thames; also called the Millennium Wheel (2000, height 135 m, diameter 120 m, supported by an A-frame on the south side only, considered the world's tallest cantilevered observation wheel, 32 ovoidal capsules (each 10 t, for 25 people)). The wheel rotates at 26 cm/s (about 0.9 km/h) so that one revolution takes about 30 minutes.

Question 13. Is harmony a human value and what is the Level 4 Management?

Response 13: The harmony is a precious human value, reflecting compatibility and accord in many areas, like feelings, actions, relationships, opinions and interests – exactly what is needed for a good advanced civilization.

Level 4 very friendly 10 Advisers of the world, who will supervise and assist the 10 L3 managers of the 10 regions of the Earth, for a total of about 7,700,000,000 people – all the people on Earth, citizens of Peaceful Terra.

Italy, Venezia, Palazzo Corner (Ca' Granda, Prefettura), north bank, 600 m west of Piazza San Marco

Question 14. Is harmony related to a state of balance, and where will the 10 Advisors be located?

Response 14: Yes, harmony means a state of balance among different ideas, with the purpose of advancing and getting better.

The L4 very friendly 10 Advisers of the world will be located each in one the ten Regions R0, R1,..., R9. For example, in the beginning, for the first month (then changing every month), the ten Advisers of the world will be located:

- in R0: Barcelona (Spain)
- in R1: Benghazi (Libya)
- in R2: Addis Ababa (Ethiopia)
- in R3: Hyderabad (Pakistan)
- in R4: Bhopal (India)
- in R5: Mandalay (Myanmar)
- in R6: Nanchong (China)
- in R7: Khabarovsk (Russia)
- in R8: Houston (USA)
- in R9: Recife (Brazil)

These ten L4 Advisers will be in permanent contact with each other, and with the L3 Advisers, for the best management of the world.

The ten L4 Advisers will move each month from a first capital of a region to the second capital of another region, at random (or based on urgency, if an emergency occurred). This mobility is essential for having a long period of tranquility and harmony.

The Advisors will be located in the current government buildings, and the excess government buildings and properties will be sold, in order to increase the budget, and to reduce the expenses.

The top 10 Advisers (and all the others) will collaborate via e-mail, telephone, videoconferences, mail, or face to face, when needed, to produce practical results for all people, very fast.

USA, New York, on 5th Ave.at E 14th St, looking southeast, The New School University Center

Question 15. How will harmony help the 10 Advisors to take decisions?

Response 15: Harmony is a sine qua non requirement for good management, because all the decisions will be by consensus only.

It is expected that the 10 Advisors are talented enough to be able to negotiate fast any disagreements between them, and quickly arrive at the best common decision, for the benefit of all people.

UK, London, From the southwest side of the Tower of London (left 180 m), looking south to the fortifications at the southwest corner of the third external western wall, and the City Hall (center left, after Thames).

Question 16. What is living in harmony and how will the 10 Advisors be elected?

Response 16: Living in peace and harmony with ourselves an all the people around means living and working together peacefully, for the benefit of all.

The ten L4 Advisers will be elected from the 10 regions, and each of them will be the First Adviser (*First among equals* – from Latin: Primus inter pares) for one month, by rotation.

The First Adviser only coordinates the work of the other 9 Advisors for one month.

Italy, Venezia, Palazzo Genovese (center), south bank of Canal Grande, 420 m west of Piazza San Marco

Question 17. How will the 10 Advisors harmoniously inform the people?

Response 17: To maintain a peaceful and harmonious atmosphere for all people, the 10 Advisers will be using a Monthly World Report.

The First Adviser, on the last day of each month, will present in writing for the world (no more than 5 standard pages) a clear and precise Monthly World Report, with a list of finished and unfinished tasks.

The other 9 Advisers will add their comments to the Monthly World Report (no more than half a page each - total report less than 9.5 pages).

In order to better know the world government, to help it, and, especially, to improve it, all able people of the world will work as volunteers at least one day per year in each of the seven departments.

After each Monthly World Report, a public opinion survey about the report should be taken, and presented to all Advisors.

All activities of the Advisors, and others from the small World Government, will be available to the people on a website.

UK, London, from the northwest corner of the Tower of London (left), looking southwest to the Shard. From around 1350 for 300 years the coronation procession started here at the Tower, ending at Westminster Abbey (4 km west (right)).

Question 18. Is harmony one of the Advisors' management responsibilities?

Response 18: Yes, harmony has a high priority for all Advisers.

The top 10 Advisers will manage Police and all other Departments.

For obvious uncooperative or improper attitude of one top Advisor X, the other 9 can replace X with X's number 2, and X will receive appropriate medical treatment.

When vacancies happen for Advisors, the number 2 for those Advisors will fill the vacancies.

All the activities of all Advisors will be recorded in computers and videos, and on paper, for people to be able to see what they are doing.

Advisors at all levels should work 40 hours/week, with 4 weeks of vacation, but many services (medical, police (firemen should be part of the police), emergency, volunteers) should be non-stop.

Advisors' compensation should be the world annual average salary (in 2019 less than $10,000) plus 4% of that world average salary, for level 4 (total $10,400), + 3 % for level 3, and so on. They all should work to increase the world average salary, in order to get themselves an increase.

All the other world government employees will have a compensation close to the average compensation of the people in the area where they are located.

All Advisors are free to speak about their administrative work, with modesty.

At least 7 of the top 10 Advisers should be present every working day.

Italy, Venezia, Palazzi Cavalli Franchetti (left) and Barbaro (center), near Ponte dell'Accademia, north bank, 720 m west of Piazza San Marco

Question 19. Is harmony excluding war?

Response 19: Certainly!

Advisors (and all the others) cannot declare war, reprisals or capture land or water.

Advisors (and all the others) cannot raise and support armies, navy, or any military forces.

UK, London: From a boat on Thames (flowing left to right), looking west to the east façade of The Royal Horseguards hotel (1884 building inspired from Château de Chambord (1547, Vallée de la Loire, Architect Domenico da Cortona), with Whitehall Gardens (from Palace of Whitehall (1240-1698) in front and Victoria Embankment (by river)

Question 20. Who will harmoniously help the management?

Response 20: Each Advisor, and each manager at all levels, will have 5 immediate assistants, who will harmoniously work together for the benefit of all people.

Each Advisor, and each manager at all levels, will have 5 immediate assistants:
1) a mathematician for finance and all other calculations,
2) a medical doctor for keeping everybody healthy, calm, polite, friendly and optimist,
3) a CEO for good management,
4) an engineer for all practical projects, and
5) a teacher for education, training and related areas.

The five assistants play a key role, because they are highly qualified professionals, who actually will carry on the practical management of the world.

The five assistants' integrity, professionalism and friendliness will significantly improve the quality of the world and local governments.

The five assistants are really the experts. They will assist the Advisors and all levels of management, in order to have an efficient, correct and professional working of the world government at all levels.

All spending proposals from Advisers must be approved by their 5 assistants (doctors, mathematicians, CEOs, engineers and teachers), and must have an already existing funding in the budget.

UK, London, from the northwest side of the Tower of London (left up), looking southeast to the three western external walls, 180 m from the Tower.

Question 21. Is understanding important for harmony, and who will oversee the top management?

Response 21: Yes, understanding other people is a generator of harmony and peace.

An Honorific World Observer will be quietly elected by direct vote – starting, for example, 1st September 2022 - for only one 3 years term, with the main duty to observe that the top 10 Advisers efficiently perform their duties, and keep their words – if they don't, they will be changed.

For managers and for everybody else, keeping their word is a serious and strict requirement.

The Honorific World Observer has this responsibility for the top 10 Advisors, but all people will pay attention to this. Words must become again important and respected.

Question 22. Are clarity and harmony important for the World Government?

Response 22: Clarity and harmony are the foundation of the World Government, because the communication with people is based on this foundation.

All the employees of the World Government are temporary, and must reapply for their positions every year.

There is no need for unions.

The World Government will be limited to:
1) the Office of the Honorific Observer (less than 10 employees),
2) the Office of the top ten Advisors (less than 100 employees), and
3) 7 small departments.

Italy, Venezia, Ponte dell'Accademia, Palazzo Cavalli Franchetti (left), Chiesa Santa Maria della Salute (back), 850 m west of Piazza San Marco

Question 23. Are work and harmony necessary for the 7 World Government Departments?

Response 23: Absolutely! All remember that work and harmony mean life, and life is work plus harmony.

The World Government will have these 7 small departments:

- Tax Department

- Collects taxes of 15% of the income of people and revenue of companies.

- The Manager of the Tax Department is appointed for a three-year term by the World 10 Advisers.

- The number of employees must be under 50,000, with excellent computers, and advanced software.

Switzerland, Geneva, from Quai Gustave Ador (1845-1928, President). Jet d'Eau (1886, 1891, 1951) – a large fountain pumping lake water at 500 liters/s to 140 m, lit up at night. It is located at the point where Lac Léman empties into the Rhône River. There are two 500 kW pumps, operating at 2,400 V, consuming one megawatt of electricity. The water leaves the nozzle (10.16 cm) at a speed of 200 km/h. At any time, there are about 7,000 liters of water in the air.

- Treasury

Treasury will control all the financial issues, including:
- antitrust
- fiscal service
- financial cooperation
- financing bank
- world reserve system
- world budget using only revenue, no borrowing, and spending only on strict necessary needs
– all the budgets, at all levels, will have a 2% surplus, which will be returned to the taxpayers
- register of all government papers and activities
- archives and records
- assist all people to have savings accounts for old age (the old age will be starting around 70), and 10% of their income should automatically go to their savings accounts. For those unable to work, their doctors and mathematicians will decide case by case.
- bankruptcies, in general, will be discouraged, and when strict necessary, will be analyzed and solved, case by case, by the doctors, mathematicians and CEOs who worked with the people who asked the bankruptcy.
- encourage all families to assist their parents, grandparents, and great-grandparents.
- housing finance
- housing for all people
- no homelessness
- consumer financial protection
- pensions
- privacy
- current social security until replaced by personal savings
- personnel management
- general services for the world government
- each the 10 regions will receive 2.5% of the world taxes - at least 30% of the money will be sent to villages and cities.
- each of the 100 sub-regions will receive 0.25% of the world taxes. At least 40% of the money will be sent to villages and cities.

- The World Central Bank will include all current central banks – starting, for example, on May 1st, 2023.

- The Special Credit Card (SCC) will be issued by the World Central Bank.

- Advisors will create a new world currency, named, for example, "coin", and all the other currencies will be exchanged for coins. The World Central Bank will implement the details.

- The counterfeiting and all other bad things, which some sick people do, will be medically treated (in specialized medical institutions when necessary), and those who did bad things will pay all the expenses, and will reimburse the victims. Victims will always be very protected, and helped to recover the losses from the attackers.

UK, London, from the Tower Millennium Pier (right down) looking southeast to Tower Bridge (1894, 244 m, 65 m height, clearance 8.6 m closed).

- People Assistance Department

It will assist people in general, including:
- parent assistance
- dispute resolution
- in very simple disputes or culpa levis (ordinary negligence, like late payments, etc.), one single assistant will decide within minutes, and all people will go back to work
- census every 5 years
- election assistance every 20 months
 - special credit cards
- people protection against abuses from anybody
- completely eliminate corruption, organized crime and drug trafficking
- all people in the world will remain in their places, and the improvements will come to them. Those who want to move to other places, will need first a special invitation from at least 10 people (not family related) where they want to move.
- all the Tribunals and related areas will be transformed in people assistance services, based on friendliness, collaboration and goodwill.
- It is well understood that no excessive bail will be required, no excessive fines imposed, no cruel and unusual punishments applied, but, at the same time, it is well understood that a person who did a bad thing will receive the necessary corrective medical treatment, and will reimburse all people who suffered damages, and the medical treatment. The victims will always receive special attention.
- Nobility (King, Prince, etc.) could continue to exist in some places, but they should not interfere with activities of the Advisors, and actually should help them.
- food safety
- trash & recycling
- free commerce
- jobs assistance
- postal service
- labor safety and harmonious relations
- land, water

- volunteers
- fitness, sport, tourism
- 10 world holidays: the normal 4 Earth events (2 solstices (around 21 June, around 21 December), and 2 equinoxes (around 21 March, around 21 September), Mother's Day on 1st May, Father's Day on 6 August, Children's Day on 6 November, Grandparents' Day on 6 February, and 2 optional days (like Thanksgiving or a Religious Day (Christmas), and New Year).

Italy, Venezia, Palazzi Nani (left), Giustinian (center& left), Ca' Foscari (right), south bank, 820 m south of Ponte Rialto.

- Medical Department

It will manage all medical and healthcare related areas, including:
- human services
- conflict resolution
- families, children, elderly
- medicine approval
- disease control and prevention
- medical doctors and assistants will make regular home visits, at least once a year, to all people, to keep them healthy, and to prevent illnesses.
- medical research: cancer, heart, lung, blood, arthritis, surgical robotics, connected computers for healthcare, etc.
- healthy homes, streets, stores, working places, etc.
- healthy aging
- all misunderstandings, disagreements or conflicts of any nature will be treated by medical personnel (with police help when strict necessary), until all is back to normal.
- no prisons are necessary, only specialized medical institutions (in simple cases, the places where the treated people live can be used, with the necessary limitations and surveillance)
- If a person X is considered that did a bad thing, X will have, within 3 days, a discussion with one or more doctors and other assistants, and will be informed of the nature and cause of the bad thing; including witnesses against and for him. Then a decision will be taken within other 3 days, by a group of doctors and other assistants. Victims of bad people will always have priority to discuss their problems with one or more doctors and other assistants, and quick decisions will be taken within 3 days, by a group of doctors and other assistants. Protection of victims has always priority.
- in order to better know the world government, to help it, and, especially, to improve it, all able people of the world will work as volunteers at least one day per year in the local facility of this department, which will have a special office for managing this volunteer work.

– all people will have government medical insurance, and they can also have private medical insurance

– there will be doctors working for the government 100%, or only part-time, or having only private practice, all with reasonable salaries and fees.

– there will be government pharmaceutical institutions and private pharmaceutical companies, offering reasonable priced medicines, without advertising to the general public.

UK, London, from the Tower Millennium Pier looking southwest to the Shard.

Italy, Venezia - The Clock Tower (Torre dell'Orologio), 1499. At the top there are two bronze figures, which strike the hours on a bell. The bell was casted at the Arsenal in 1497. Below is the winged lion of Venice. There was a statue of the Doge Agostino Barbarigo (Doge 1486-1501) before the lion. Below the statues of the Virgin and Child. On either side are two large blue panels showing the time: 5:55 PM, the same on the clock below: XVII very close to XVIII.

- Police

Police will provide assistance for:
- accidents
- disasters
- complete elimination of nuclear, chemical and biological arms, firearms and explosives
- world complete security
- world cooperation
- conflict reduction and resolution
- investigations
- emergency assistance
- training
- delinquency prevention in general, and especially juvenile
- protection of Advisors, important government buildings, etc.
- extended surveillance and reconnaissance to prevent bad events
- fire protection
- volunteers to help police
- police will be present at public meetings, services, shows, etc., in order to protect the public
- public order
- ensuring traffic safety
- completely eliminate corruption, organized crime and drug trafficking
- movement of people based on civilized rules
- assist and protect those who have encountered violence
- World Police and specialists from the former United Nations and Interpol will be ready and very mobile for urgent and special operations, when they are needed.
- Police will be the only department which will have some small arms, in order to stop some very bad people (who are very sick).
- a small manufacturing and maintenance of arms unit will be part of the Police Department, under strict control.
- Police will work with medical personnel, mathematicians, CEOs, engineers, teachers and others, to make sure that all the people on the Planet are in good mental health, in order to prevent bad situations. This is also a major responsibility of all Advisors.

- prevention of bad events
- The Advisors will allocate the necessary budget for Police, and Police will assist people in need.

UK, London, on the boat Hurricane Clipper, going upstream, looking southeast to the right bank, at the University of Greenwich, Trinity Laban Conservatoire of Music and Dance (center right), and Chapel at the Old Royal Naval College (center left).

- Education Department

- Over 2 billions of children in the world will get a solid peace-oriented education, to give a solid peace-oriented foundation for a good, free, peaceful and prosperous life.
- Education is very important – teachers will work with parents and grandparents, to educate the children to leave healthy in a sustainable peace, liberty and prosperity.
- Discipline must be strict, and those who do not behave properly, will get medical assistance.
- The world will have 4 school levels (SLs) of education:
SL1 – Kindergarten – 2 years: age 5 and 6
SL2 – Primary School – 4 years: age 7, 8, 9 and 10
SL3 – Secondary School – 3 years: age 11, 12 and 13
SL4 – High School or Vocational School – 4 years: age 14, 15, 16 and 17
- A World Library will include the Library of Congress and all the other great libraries – they will remain where they are now, but will be digitally interconnected, and accessible from any place in the world.
- adult education: technical, career
- training for employment
- management training
- post high school education
- peace education
- world constitution education

USA, New York, on Broadway at Chambers St: City Hall Park (left down), New York by Gehry (left, or Beekman Tower, 76-story, 271 m, 2011, Deutsche Bank Bldg. (center up), Woolworth Bldg. (1913, 241 m, right up).

- Science & Technology Department.

It will help in the areas of:
- mathematics
- statistics
- science
- technology
- Algorithmic Governance will be an essential tool for a better and impartial governing of the world, used by the Advisers elected by people. Mathematicians from all countries will work to improve the Algorithmic Governance, to better serve the people.
- cyberspace complete security will be achieved and strictly maintained
- information systems
- computer services
- Internet
- scientific cooperation
- economic development at the world level
- infrastructure improvement and maintenance at the world level
- innovation and improvements in all areas, at the world level
- transportation at the world level
- safety
- security
- aviation
- highway
- cars
- railroads without noise
- maritime administration
- logistics
- strategic planning at the world level
- public works
- fleet maintenance
- standards: weights, measures, etc.
- research at the world level
- risk analysis
- laboratories
- engineering

- communications at the world level
- telecommunications
- networks
- peaceful nuclear energy use at the world level
- safety
- waste
- electrical power
- oceanic analysis at the world level
- atmospheric analysis at the global level
- meteorological service and prognosis at the global level
- world resources analysis
- sustainable use of world resources
- geographical and geological activity
- product safety at the global level
- hazardous material and chemical safety
- government broadcasting (radio, tv, Internet, newspaper, etc.) including news, scientific and technical information
- private broadcasting will continue, but the world government must be able to directly inform the people, without intermediaries
- space exploration and expansion at the world level – very important for the future
- patent and trademark
- intellectual rights
- all government work, which can be done by private companies, will be contracted with the best and reasonably priced private companies. At the same time, the government should always have competitive services for people – from plumbing and electrical help, to mortgage and buying or selling a house.

Italy, Venezia - Libreria Sansoviniana (left), Il Campanile (center-left), Palazzo Ducale (right), and a Japanese couple wedding picture.

Question 24. What is the frequency of harmonious elections?

Response 24: Yes, harmonious elections will take place every 20 months:

The Advisers should be elected every 20 months for one term only. If an Adviser X was elected for a term T1, then the next term T2 will have another Advisor Y. For the next term T3, X can be elected again, but the next term T4 will have a new Adviser, and so on. All levels of Advisers (minimum age 25 years) can be elected, not consecutively, at most 4 times (maximum 80 months = 6 years and 8 months).

All the employees in Government will respect Seneca's (circa 1,960 years ago) aphorism "To govern is to serve, not to rule", and Hippocrates' (over 2,400 years ago) aphorism "Make a habit of two things: to help; or at least to do no harm."

Advisers should have exceptional results obtained from their work, and based on these results, plus modesty, moderation, good character, friendliness, sharp mind, wisdom, good morals, and intense desire to help people, they will be elected, without any campaigning, publicity, fundraising, donations, debates, propaganda, political parties, advertising, or similar activities.

There will be use of advanced digital technology, which opens up entirely new opportunities for developing direct elections, and public control of the institutions, improving the transparency of the election procedure, and taking into account the interests and opinions of each voter (over the age of 21, who are not in a special medical institution for bad behavior or for mental health).

UK, London, on the boat Hurricane Clipper, going upstream (against the flow), looking west to the left (north) bank, with Ontario Tower (apartments, center right, with oblique roof).

Question 25. Is there a serious checking of harmony as part of qualifications?

Response 25: Yes, there is an Election Commission, which will make sure that all candidates have the talent to work in harmony with all people.:

An Election Commission of 110 representatives from the 10 regions and from the 100 sub-regions, elected separately for 5 years, will have to examine the qualifications of all the candidates for Advisers, and for other senior management positions. Unqualified candidates will be asked to improve their qualifications, and then to try again later.

It is important to refresh the management, and to bring new people to help the big family of 7.7 B people. The older generations, who performed well, will be retained in important roles, because experience and maturity count very much. At least two months before the retirement, they will kindly be asked to transfer their expertise to the younger generation. Even after retirement, they will occasionally be invited to share their expertise.

In every election, with every winner, will be other two for number 2 and number 3. The number 2 and number 3 for each management position will be used when number 1 is not available (vacation, sick, etc.). They will constantly work for number 1, helping to solve urgent problems for the people.

Good elections are essential for the future.
There has been a tendency to make elections conflict generating events, with lots of propaganda, false information, heavy donations, unpolite confrontations, bully fundraising, hostile political parties and organizations, unlimited power ambitions, etc.
This will be completely changed into clean, friendly elections, in which people choose between leaders with outstanding

results, plus talent to lead people to peace and freedom, modesty, moderation, good character, friendliness, sharp mind, wisdom, good morals, and intense desire to help people – no campaigning, no publicity, no fundraising, no donations, no debates, no propaganda, no political parties, no advertising, or similar activities.

All Advisors should also be local Administrators – they must show that they are good managers, and produce practical results for all people.

USA, Cape Cod, Highland Museum & Lighthouse, at 27 Highland Light Rd, North Truro, 10 km east of Provincetown, northeast of Cape Cod.

Question 26. Will the people be harmoniously consulted?

Response: Of course, friendly referendum every three months, because the world is a harmonious family of over 7.7 billions of people:

An electronic world referendum will be organized every three months. The main questions will be:

1. Are you satisfied with the Government?
2. What Government work is good?
3. What Government work is not good?
4: Suggestions for improvement:

Within two months after each referendum, the Government will respond to the people. Based on the suggestions received, new pro-people rules will be replacing some old rules.

UK, London, from a boat on Thames, looking northwest to new residential buildings, near Blackwall train station and Billingsgate Market

Question 27. Can you have harmony with arms?

Response: No way – there will be no arms at all, because arms are used to dominate others, not to have harmony:

Arms will not exist anymore, and only the police will have some small arms. Those who want arms for hunting or sport, will borrow them from police stations, with proper documents, rules and payments.

All military units will become strong civilian organizations, working to improve the quality of life for everybody.

For practical reasons, the transition from the current imperfect situation to the much better Sustainable Peace and Prosperity Structure (SPPS) will be very smooth: first - all the countries remain as they are, and they will begin – for example on January 1st, 2022 - to negotiate total and complete disarmament, with the help of the United Nations, for 3 months. Then for 5 months will intensely work to eliminate all the arms – either transform them in peaceful tools, or destroy them. Then a continuous verification and monitoring will be implemented, the make sure that the world finally achieved complete disarmament forever!

Question 28. Is census important for harmony?

Response: Certainly, census is also important for delimitations, special cards, the compassion for those in need, etc.

A census will take place every 5 years – starting, for example, on October 1st, 2023 - and all people will receive a special credit card (SCC), with their photo and other personal data. The delimitations between regions, and between sub-regions, will be adjusted by the census.

Italy, Cividale del Friuli: 3 Nov 2009, on Corso Paolino d'Aquileia, on the bridge of Iacopo da Bissone (1442, 50 m by 3.6 m, height 22.5 m, rock) over Natisone River (flowing from back to front), 150 m southeast of Palazzo Comunale, looking northeast to il Campanile of Monastero Santa Maria in Valle (650, up left) and Natisone River.

Question 29. Will people have some helping cards, to have a harmonious life?

Response: Definitively!

The special credit card (SCC) will be used to buy everything, to identify for voting, for census, for travel, for medical assistance, etc.

The current private credit cards will continue to work as usual.

The changes of the delimitations between regions, and also sub-regions, will be inputted on these cards, and no other work is needed.

USA, New York, on W 46th St, looking southeast, 100 m northwest of the Times Square (center), Marquis Theatre (right

Question 30. For harmony, who are sacred for people?

Response: People!

People are something sacred for people

The enemies of the people on Earth are not other people, but viruses, microbes, bad bacteria and hundreds of deadly illnesses – all people on Earth will work together, in a harmonious effort, against these real enemies for all of us.

UK, London, from a boat on Thames, looking to the cable car (2012, 1,100 m, elevation 90 m, speed 6 m/s) over Thames, between North Greenwich Peninsula (west) and the Royal Docks (east).

Question 31. Will non-violence and harmony be the rule?

Response: Yes, very clearly, we need harmonious relationships between all people.:

Non-violence is a strict requirement for all activities on Earth.

The first rule for everybody on Earth comes from the Hippocratic Oath: Primum non nocere - first do not harm.

USA, New York, Broadway (left straight) at West 4th Street (to the right, where the New York University Courant Institute of Mathematical Sciences (founder Richard Courant (1888-1972), in 1935), and New York University Physics Department are located).

Question 32. Will the doctors be closer to people and promote harmony?

Response: Categorically! Home visits will be the real joy, and will be full of harmony.

Medical doctors and assistants will make regular home visits to all people, to keep them healthy, and to prevent illnesses.

Italy, Venezia, Palazzi Mocenigo (left, north bank), Ca' Rezzonico (center-left, south bank), Nani, Giustinian, Ca' Foscari and Balbi (right).

Question 33. Will the truth resurface, to help harmony?

Response: No question about it – harmony also means to have similar goals, therefore the truth is always needed!

People need only truth in order to create a long term peaceful and harmonious society.

If someone lies – medical treatment will follow.

UK, London, from a boat on Thames, looking west to the center of Canary Wharf, with the HSBC building (2002, center right, Canada Square, 200 m

France, the upper part of the western façade of Cathédrale Notre Dame de Paris (1163 – 1345, 90 m), on the south-eastern part of the Île de la Cité, which is considered the center of Paris, in the fourth arrondissement. The organ has 7,374 pipes, with about 900 classified as historical. It has 110 real stops, five 56-key manuals and a 32-key pedalboard; it is now fully computerized. The Towers at Notre-Dame contain five church bells. The great bourdon bell, Emmanuel, from 1681, 13 t, is located in the South Tower (right).

Question 34. How important is freedom for a harmonious society?

Response: It is fundamental for all people – freedom and harmony go hand in hand, you cannot have harmony without freedom.

Freedom is a fundamental requirement on Earth.

It is well understood that this freedom refers to doing good things in a civilized manner, not for war, violence or similar bad things, which are against the wellbeing of the people.

Freedom goes hand in hand with responsibility.

People can assemble peacefully only.

Italy, Venezia, Palazzi Barbarigo (right), Pisani Mor (center), Tiepolo (center-left), Persogo (left), south bank, 520 m south of Ponte Rialto.

Question 35. To have harmony, how will the economy be?

Response: Free market economy, with harmony - not perfect, but it will be improved.

For economy it is clear that the free market economy, while not perfect, gives the best results, but all people will have the option to choose between friendly private services, and friendly government services. Independent assistants and monitors will make sure that there are no abuses. Sine qua non requirements for happiness are morality and free market.

From a boat on Thames, looking east to The O2 Arena, or North Greenwich Arena, a multi-purpose indoor riverside arena (2007, capacity 20,000, 2 km north of the Royal Observatory Greenwich).

Question 36. What about religion and harmony?

Response: Religion will be free, and will help people, because usually religion promotes harmony.

The religion should be free, and is expected not to interfere with activities of the Advisors, and actually should help people.

USA, New York, Broadway at Washington Place, with New York University buildings.

Question 37. To have harmony, can people petition the World Government?

Response: Certainly, and the people can change the government, if it does not promote harmony.

People of course can petition the small Word Government, and can change it anytime, if it does not perform as expected.

Italy, Venezia, Palazzi Querini (left), Grimani (center), Layard (center-left) and Barbarigo (left), south bank, 470 m south of Ponte Rialto.

Question 38. Will finally spending be less than revenue, for maintaining harmony?

Response: Yes, indeed – if there is deficit, the harmony disappears:

All budgets will have a surplus of 2% - there will be a strict application of the Latin aphorism: "Sumptus censum ne superset" (Let not your spending exceed your income).

UK, Greenwich, from Royal Observatory Greenwich (1676), looking northwest to the National Maritime Museum, University of Greenwich, tall buildings after Thames (left), in Canary Wharf, the Shard (left

Question 39. Will old and new errors be eliminated, with emotional harmony?

Response: Without question, it is a burning issue, and emotional harmony will certainly help:

Correcting errors is a permanent duty for everybody - Darwin (over 140 years ago, around 1880) said "To kill an error is as good a service as, and sometimes even better than, the establishing of a new truth or fact."

USA, Cape Cod, on the MacMillan Pier (600 m southeast from Pilgrim Monument), Boston Fast Ferries from Provincetown.

Question 40. Wherever there is a human being, there is an opportunity for what?

Response: A kindness! We all remember Seneca - kindness is required for harmony:

Kindness is a requirement for everybody.

Seneca (over 1,960 years ago, circa 4 BC – 65 AD, 69) said "Wherever there is a human being, there is an opportunity for a kindness."

This is a fundamental idea which must be constantly applied.

Italy, Rome: Accademia Nazionale dei Lincei (1603) in Villa Farnesina (1510). The author was invited to give a lecture here in 1977.

UK, Greenwich, on Gagarin (First Man in Space) Terrace, on the southwest part of the South Building (1899) of the Royal Observatory Greenwich (1676), looking northeast to the south part of the west side (right), the west part of the south side (left), and to the statue of Yuri Gagarin (1934-1968, Russian cosmonaut, the first man to journey into space, with Vostok spacecraft, which completed an orbit (1h 48') of the Earth on 12 April 1961. Resting place: Kremlin Wall Necropolis.

Question 41. Will the Government be fixed in some big buildings, with no harmony?

Response: No way, all levels of government will be highly mobile – this mobility will bring harmony to all places on Earth:

All levels of government will be highly mobile - changing of the capitals for the 10 regions, and for the 100 sub-regions, etc.

It is necessary to move the government close to the people, to be able to quickly solve the local problems.

Locally the people will decide how to better organize themselves, to be more efficient and harmonious, with the help of the world government when necessary. Like in any big family, there will be differences in organization and management, based on their abilities and objectives, but all must be peaceful and harmonious. Conflicts will be promptly resolved by the medical personnel, police, and other assistants.

Italy, Cividale del Friuli: 3 Nov 2009, on the left bank of the Natisone River (flowing from right to left), at the southeast end of the bridge of Iacopo da Bissone (1442, 50 m by 3.6 m, height 22.5 m, rock), 200 m southeast of Palazzo Comunale, looking to the northeast side of the bridge and the right bank of the river, with il Campanile (up right) of il Duomo di Santa Maria Assunta (1457-1529).

Question 42. In a Harmonious Society, what will the World Police role be?

Response: To help people and to promote harmony everywhere:

The United Nations will change in 2-3 years (for example, by 2024) into World Police and Assistance Organization (WPAO), to help local police in case of big natural disasters or big accidents, and will report to the top 10 Advisers. They will be located in all capitals, and help the locals. When an emergency appears, they will quickly move to solve the emergency.

The police powers will be limited, and they will know and be friend with all the people in their jurisdiction – this is the key element of a civilized and peaceful Earth. If they notice a person with bad intentions, they immediately retain that person and call for a medical assistant (and other assistants, if necessary), to analyze and solve the issue very quickly.

Police will be people's friends everywhere, and they will always help people.

Prevention of bad events is the main objective of everybody. If a bad event occurs, the police and their assistants will eliminate the consequences, reestablish the normal situation, and determine why the bad event occurred, in order to improve their activity, and prevent such bad events in the future.

Private property cannot be taken for public use, without just compensation, decided by at least 5 assistants.

A person cannot deprive another person of life, liberty, or property, which, unfortunately, occurs very frequently in the world, and very much effort and energy will be allocated to prevent such bad events.

In order to prevent bad things, the police, doctors and their assistants will be in permanent contact with all the people, by visiting them, phone calls, e-mails, tele-videos, and mail, to keep everybody calm and happy.

UK, Greenwich, the north side of the Royal Observatory (1676); between the two vertical white lines on the house, a white plaque with a red vertical line shows the Prime Meridian (0) of the world, east is to the left, west to the right. From the round hole above, a powerful green laser is shining north in the night, since 1999.

Question 43. In a harmonious world, will the World Government be open all the time?

Response: Yes, about 66% of the Government will always be working somewhere on the Earth - if people need help, they can always call the Government – this is the key to a harmonious society:

About 66% of the people of the world are working at any moment. Therefore, non-stop working of all world government departments – especially medical, police, emergency, volunteers – will be carefully organized.

Italy, Venezia, Palazzi Persigo (right, north bank), Marcello di Leoni (center), Dandolo-Paolucci (center-left), Civran-Grimani (left), 700 m sPR..

Question 44. What about privacy and harmony?

Response: Privacy of negotiations and discussions are necessary, while harmony ties people together:

In order to have serious and constructive discussions and negotiations, they must be private.

Privacy and discipline are necessary for good government work.

The results will be public and preserved, but not the private discussions.

UK, London, from Peter Harrison Planetarium (2007, right), looking south to the west part of the north side of the Astronomy Center (1899).

Question 45. Will the Government be polite and harmonious?

Response: You bet!

It is a strict requirement for the top management, and for all others, to be highly civilized, polite, courteous, harmonious and efficient.

Who wants to work for the world government must have good manners.

Harmony in the world starts from the harmony and good manners of the people in the world government.

Because all people on Earth want to live in harmony right now, it will be relatively easy to implement this in one good and civilized country. This may include having small, beautiful and commonly agreed fences around properties, because good fences make good neighbors, and also helps with more privacy.

Question 46. Will the conflicts remain for long, with no harmony?

Response: No, all conflicts must not only be quickly resolved, but they also must be transformed in friendships – this is necessary in order to maintain harmony:

The medical personnel and others will work diligently to make sure that disputes are resolved, and then a friendship is developed. Only in this way the situation will become stable.

People want peace, freedom, health, friendship and prosperity, therefore conflicts should be quickly resolved, and then the corrective medical treatment will include the transformation of hostility and aggressiveness into harmony and friendship.

Dispute resolution is not only Government's obligation, but it will be everybody's duty.

There will be professional assistance from medical personnel, police, people assistance specialists, volunteers, religious organizations, and many others, but the bottom line is that everybody must avoid disputes.

When there are different opinions, just stay calm, express your opinion, listen to others, and continue calm the discussion until a compromise is reached.

There is no need to spend much time and energy – let the people decide, and even if your idea is not temporarily accepted, there are chances that in the future you'll have more people agree with you.

UK, Greenwich, Peter Harrison (born 1937) Planetarium (2007, 120-seat digital laser planetarium), to the right Main Entrance, The Meridian Line, Flamsteed House (1676), Meridian Observatory.

Question 47. How will the people harmoniously communicate?

Response: Using a common language and alphabet:

As a single big, over 7.7 B, family on Earth, all people must be able to communicate easily with each other.

For this reason, a common language and alphabet on Earth are needed. Because English is a de facto common language now, it will be taken as the basis of the world language, let's call it Mundo, which will be taught in all schools, and used in the world government. All the other languages will continue as secondary languages.

The same is true for the Latin alphabet, which will be used everywhere, with other alphabets as secondary.

The teachers will have a very significant role in implementing this idea.

Italy, Venezia, Palazzo Dona on the south bank, 450 m south from Ponte Rialto

Question 48. In a global harmony, what about the global wealth?

Response: It will be carefully used only for peace, freedom and prosperity for all – the global wealth will surely help harmony in the world:

The 2018 Global Wealth Report from Credit Suisse shows that the total global wealth has reached $317 trillions (circa $41,000/person), which is encouraging, and all this wealth must be used only for peace.

Like in any big family, there are differences, because some work more, some spend less, some move faster, and, especially, some are sick – this is the main reason for differences: not all people can be equally sick, some people are sicker than others. However, all the people and the government will work to help each other.

It is a major responsibility of the Government to increase the global wealth, and to train those in need, to have better working abilities and opportunities.

UK, Greenwich, northeast side of the British tea clipper ship Cutty Sark (1869, out of service 1954, volume 2,725 m³, weight (displacement) 2,100 t at 6.1 m depth (draught), length 85 m, beam (width) 11 m, sail 3,000 m², speed 32 km/h, capacity to transport 1,700 t, crew 30).

Question 49. Will the bureaucracy dominate as always, or will it be replaced with harmony?

Response: the goal is no bureaucracy whatsoever, and plenty of harmony everywhere!

No bureaucracy – this is required by all people, and every day attention will be given for improvements in this direction.

In a well-organized country, with all people working together in harmony, this can be accomplished in several years.

Constant attention will be focused on avoiding duplication at all levels of the world government – there must be continuous collaboration between all levels, to prevent duplication, and to eliminate it, if it was found.

A vice is nourished by being concealed (from Latin: Alitur vitium vivitque tegendo).

Question 50. Will corruption generate new problems again, or will the harmony win?

Response: Clearly no corruption, and only harmony around!

Everybody will work really hard to completely eliminate corruption, organized crime and drug trafficking.

Italy, Venezia, Palazzo Rava (center), on Fondamenta del Vin Castello, south bank, 250 m south of Ponte Rialto.

Question 51. Will people get good interest on their savings, to have harmonious life?

Response: 5%.

Each government department will have some reserves for special situations (natural disasters, big accidents), and the banks will also have good financial reserves.

All people will be encouraged to save some money in banks with 5% interest.

UK, Greenwich, from the right bank of Thames looking southeast to the northwest entrance of Greenwich Pier, 10 Km southeast from Tower Bridge.

Question 52. In a harmonious society, is there concern regarding integrity and efficiency?

Response: Sure – inspectors will help – harmony implies integrity and efficiency.

Inspectors will help the Government with the integrity and efficiency issues – always there are ways to improve the work.

Inspectors will give advice regarding integrity and efficiency, and will take corrective actions when necessary.

Paris (250 BC): l'Hôtel de Ville (City Hall since 1357, King Francis I started this building in 1533, finished 1628, 1873-1892

Question 53. Will family assistance have priority?

Response: Yes, everybody wants harmonious families.

Because all families need assistance from time to time, and the big 7.7 B family on Earth contains billions of small families, all of them will have the assistance they need – this will be the result of one country well organized and managed.

USA, Boston: 3 Dec 2009, the northeast façade of the Harvard Medical School Anno Domini 1904, founded in 1782, the graduate medical school of Harvard University, 1660 students, acceptance rate 3.7%. Harvard University: 7,200 undergraduates; 14,000 Graduates, 4,671 Faculty members; 152 Nobel laureates are members of Harvard University, 12 Schools and 2 Institutes for Advanced Studies, including Harvard School of Engineering and Applied Sciences, $32.3 billion endowment. $4.2 billion budget).

Question 54. Will abuses continue or will harmony win?

Response: Certainly not abuses, and much more harmony – it is a demanding effort, after thousands of years of all kinds of abuses, but the abuses will be gone!

Special attention will be given by Advisors to avoid abuses and wrong interpretations of the rules. All assistants (doctors, mathematicians, CEOs, engineers and teachers) will closely monitor all activities, to avoid abuses and wrong interpretations of the rules.

This requirement of not having abuses is demanding – but this is a general job, not only for Government, but for everybody, as part of the big family, we just don't need abuses.

The abuse, in some places, of confiscating the land by some government bureaucrats will be eliminated – the land belongs to the people, not the government.

The abuse, in some places, of having trains, airplanes, and others making unhealthy noises, with the government support, will be eliminated – peoples' health has always priority.

The abuse, in some places, of having to change the clocks twice a year will be eliminated – only the normal local time zones will be used.

If abuses are observed, they will be immediately reported to the Government, and corrected, in general, by the People Assistance Department, which will have personnel, including medical assistants, to analyze and promptly solve the abuses.

Question 55. What about commerce and harmony?

Response: Naturally there will be intense free commerce based on harmony.

In one country, with one market, the commerce between the people on Earth will be free of taxes, tariffs, duties, etc. – plenty of opportunities for everybody.

Italy, Roma - Arco di Costantino (312, left), and Amphitheatrum Flavium (Colosseum, 80 AD, right), from Via di San Gregorio.

Question 56. Will the speech be free and responsible?

Response: Yes, the speech will be free and very responsible.

The speech will be free and responsible. It is expected not to call for war, violence, or similar destructive activities. People want peace, freedom, health, friendship, harmony and prosperity.

France, Paris: Rue Soufflot (from Panthéon, looking north-west to Jardin du Luxembourg (1612, back), and Tour Eiffel (1889, 324 m)), with the Université Paris 1 Panthéon-Sorbonne (1150, 1971, right).

Question 57. Will the press be free and responsible?

Response: Yes, the press will be free and responsible – it is expected that the press will help the people and promote harmony.

The press will be free and responsible. It is expected not to call for war, violence, or similar destructive activities. People want peace, freedom, health, friendship, harmony and prosperity.

Italy, 6 April 1978, Pisa, Cattedrale di Pisa (1092, striped-marble, left), Torre di Pisa (August 1173-1372, 55.86 m on the low side, 56.67 m on the high side, white-marble, 296 steps, right).

Question 58. Will some people be able to protest violently?

Response: No - people can assemble peacefully only. If some disagree with a decision, they can always inform the government, which will respond in 3 days. The discussion will continue with calm and respect, until everything is clarified.

People can assemble peacefully only, with police for help. It is expected not to call for war, violence, or similar destructive activities. People want peace, freedom, health, friendship, harmony and prosperity.

UK, London, on Thames looking northwest to nice residential buildings on Wapping Wall, east of Shadwell Basin. 2 km east of Tower Bridge

Question 59. Will everybody have a job?

Response: Yes – there will be more jobs than people, in order to support harmony.

There will always be plenty of jobs at world minimum wage (assisting other people, for example), and the standard situation will be this: more jobs than available people, so people will choose the jobs they like the most.

Italy, 6 April 1978, Pisa, Palazzo della Carovana (1562-1564) now for Scuola Normale Superiore (1810, by Napoleon Bonaparte (1769-1821), 460 students, 6% admission rate, best in Italy).

Question 60. Will beggars be everywhere?

Response: No - no unemployment, no homelessness, no begging, no tipping, just peace, harmony and prosperity.

No unemployment, no homelessness, no begging – just all working harmoniously, having good houses, and helping each other.

USA, New York, on W 42nd St, the northeast façade of the New York Public Library

UK, London, on Thames looking north to Oliver's Wharf, a luxury residential building on Wapping High Street, parallel to the river.

Question 61. How can the World Constitution be improved?

Response: When 66% of the voters agree to have more harmony, more collaboration, etc.

This Constitution of the World can be improved when over 66% of the voters agree.

Obviously, there will appear in the future many more advanced technologies, medicines, etc., which will certainly create conditions to have more harmony, more collaboration, etc.

Italy, Venezia, Fermata San Silvestro and Palazzo Barzizza (center and left), south bank, 300 m south of Ponte Rialto.

USA, New York, on West 34th St, looking northwest, Empire State Building (left

Question 62. What is the purpose of the people on Earth?

Response: To be healthy, to live in peace, freedom and harmony, to be prosperous, and to prepare to expand to the Moon, asteroids, Mars, etc.

The purpose for all people on Earth is to be healthy, to live in peace, freedom and harmony, to be prosperous, and to prepare to expand to the Moon, asteroids, Mars, and other places in the Universe, which can support life.

UK, London, on Thames looking north to Sky Garden bld (up right, 2014, 155 m, 35 floors), Tower 42 (center back, 1981, 183 m), and Old Billingsgate (1875, center right, events venue, former fish market).

Question 63. Are there immediate objectives for people?

Response: Yes, reserve time for happiness and harmony, etc.:

Important immediate objectives for everybody are:
- Reserve time for happiness.
- Use robots and automated processes, work less, and spend more time with your family.
- The weekend will be like a small vacation.
- Prevent burnout.
- Make civilized behavior and harmony everywhere is an important issue.
- Eliminate stress.
- Help friends and colleagues.
- Keep everybody relaxed, calm, friendly, patient, and happy.

.

Question 64. How do you harmonize the world?

Response: Using cordiality, having peaceful discussions, using a balanced approach to all issues, being amicable, coordinating the work in teams, being pleasant and melodic, etc.

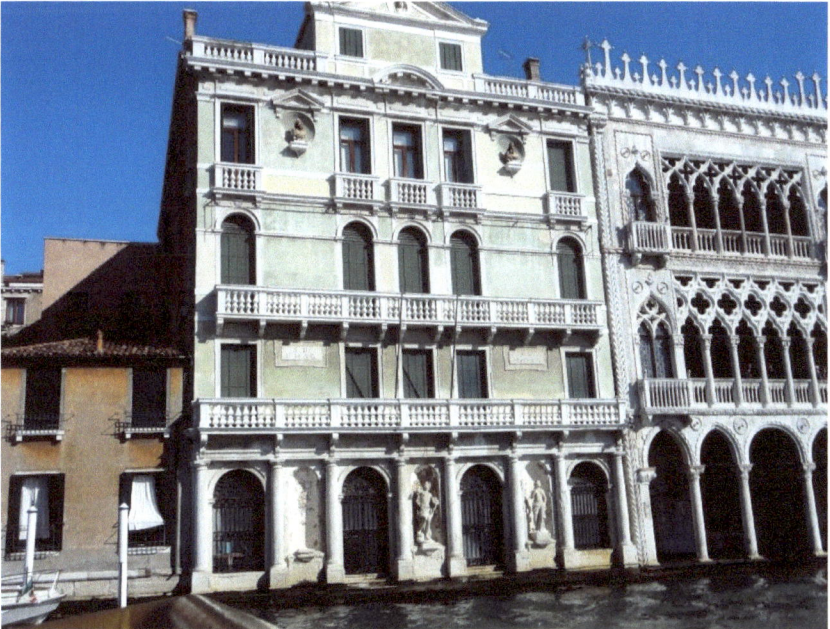

Italy, Venezia, Ca' D'Oro (right) and a palazzo with statues built in 1766 (center), north bank, 580 m east of Ponte degli Scalzi.

Question 65. Are there books for better understanding this harmony and Constitution?

Response: Certainly:

For better understanding and easier implementation of this harmony and the World Constitution, the following books, by Michael M. Dediu, are recommended:
- Our Future is Sustainable Peace and Prosperity – Moving from conflicts to harmony and peace
– Our Future Depends on Good World Educations – Moving from frail education to solid education.
– Friendly, Helpful & Smart World Management - Moving from bureaucracy to responsive world management
– If You Want Peace, Prepare for Peace! – Moving from preparation for war to preparation for peace
– World with One Country & its Ten Friendly Regions - Moving from 195 disagreeing countries, to 1 country with 10 collaborating regions
– After 10,000 Years of Conflicts, People want 10,000 Years of Harmony - Moving from continuous wars to stable peace
- The Constitution of the World – Moving from many unsustainable constitutions, to just one Constitution of the World
- World Constitution Implementation – Moving from violent changes, to smooth transition to the Constitution of the World
- It is getting truer and truer – we urgently need the World Constitution: Moving from anarchic changes, to balanced transition to the Constitution of the World
- World Constitution with Lovely Comments - Moving from many suboptimal constitutions to the much better Constitution of the World

USA, Bretton Woods, the southeast corner of the Mount Washington Resort (1902, elevation 500 m, by Joseph Stickney (1840 – 1903, coal business)), where the documents of the United Nations Monetary and Financial Conference (1 – 22 July 1944, 730 delegates from 44 Allied nations, at Bretton Woods (12 km west of Mount Washington (1917 m), 250 km north of Boston), established the International Monetary Fund and the World Bank. The Bretton Woods system worked for 27 years, until 1971) were signed.

Question 66. For what territories is this Constitution full of harmony intended?

Response: For all Earth, the space around Earth, for the Moon, Mars, asteroids, etc.

The Constitution of the World is valid not only on Earth, but also on the space around Earth, on the Moon, Mars, asteroids and any other places where the very good people on Earth will be moving in the future.

UK, London, on Thames looking northwest to Southwark Bridge (center left) and St Paul's Cathedral (1675-1697-1711, height 111 m, length 158 m).

Question 67. How long will this World Constitution be harmoniously working?

Response: For at least 10,000 years of harmonious living

The Constitution of the World is intended for at least 10,000 years of harmonious living on the happy Earth and many other places.

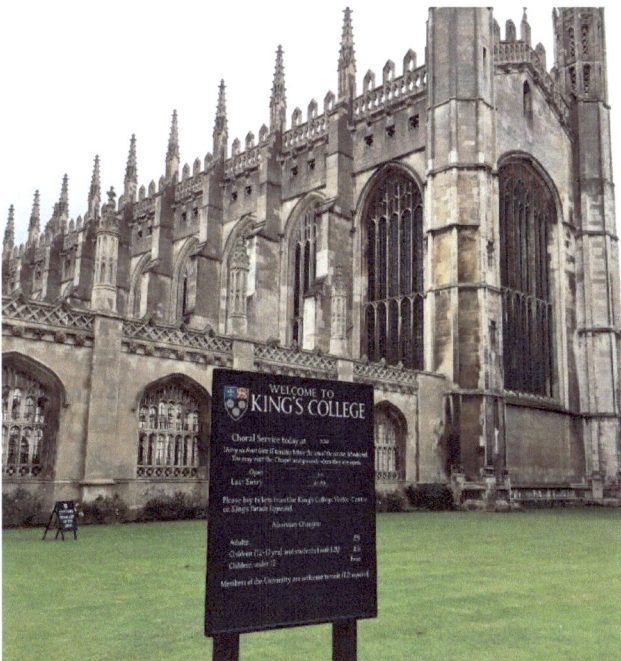

UK, Cambridge, from the entrance to King's College (1441), looking northwest to the Chapel (the south façade (center left), and the east façade (right)).

Question 68. When will this Constitution be ready to come harmoniously into force?

Response: On 6 March 2020.

The Constitution of the World is ready to come into force, and to be put into practice, for the benefit of all people on Earth, on 6 March 2020, and it is ready to remain into force, and enjoyed by all people, at least until 6 March 12020.

Italy, Venezia, Palazzo Michiel di Colonne (center-right), north bank.

Bibliography

Michael M. Dediu is also the author of these books (which can be found on Amazon.com, and www.derc.com):

1. Aphorisms and quotations – with examples and explanations
2. Axioms, aphorisms and quotations – with examples and explanations
3. 100 Great Personalities and their Quotations
4. Professor Petre P. Teodorescu – A Great Mathematician and Engineer
5. Professor Ioan Goia – A Dedicated Engineering Professor
6. Venice (Venezia) – a new perspective. A short presentation with photographs
7. La Serenissima (Venice) - a new photographic perspective. A short presentation with many photos
8. Grand Canal – Venice. A new photographic viewpoint. A short presentation with many photos
9. Piazza San Marco – Venice. A different photographic view. A short presentation with many photos
10. Roma (Rome) - La Città Eterna. A new photographic view. A short presentation with many photos
11. Why is Rome so Fascinating? A short presentation with many photos
12. Rome, Boston and Helsinki. A short photographic presentation
13. Rome and Tokyo – two captivating cities. A short photographic presentation
14. Beautiful Places on Earth – A new photographic presentation
15. From Niagara Falls to Mount Fuji via Rome - A novel photographic presentation
16. From the USA and Canada to Italy and Japan - A fresh photographic presentation
17. Paris – Why So Many Call This City Mon Amour - A lovely photographic presentation

18. The City of Light – Paris (La Ville-Lumière) - A kaleidoscopic photographic presentation

19. Paris (Lutetia Parisiorum) – the romance capital of the world - A kaleidoscopic photographic view

20. Paris and Tokyo – a joyful photographic presentation. With a preamble about the Universe

UK, London, on Thames (flowing left to right), looking northeast to the steel suspension London Millennium Footbridge (1996-2000, 325 m).

Italy, Rome (753 BC, one of the oldest continuously occupied cities in Europe, called Roma Aeterna (The Eternal City) and Caput Mundi (Capital of the World)), in Piazza Quirinale, the northeast side of Fountain of Castor (1818), with Obelisco del Quirinale (or Monte Cavallo, 1786, 29 m, from Mausoleum of Augustus (63 BC-14 AD)), and statues of the Dioscuri (Castor and Pollux, twin sons of Zeus and Leda) from the thermal baths of Constantine (272-337), Opus Phidiai on the left.

21. From USA to Japan via Canada – A cheerful photographic documentary

22. 200 Wonderful Places, In The Last 50 Years – A personal photographic documentary

23. Must see places in USA and Japan - A kaleidoscopic photographic documentary

24. Grandeurs of the World - A kaleidoscopic photographic documentary

25. Corneliu Leu – writer on the same wavelength as Mark Twain. An American viewpoint

26. From Berkeley to Pompeii via Rome – A kaleidoscopic photographic documentary

27. From America to Europe via Japan - A kaleidoscopic photographic documentary

28. Discover America and Japan - A photographic documentary

29. J. R. Lucas – philosopher on a creative parallel with Plato, An American viewpoint

30. From America to Switzerland via France - A photographic documentary

31. From Bretton Woods to New York via Cape Cod - A photographic documentary

32. Splendid Places on the Atlantic Coast of the U. S. A. - A photographic documentary

33. Fourteen nice Cities on three Continents - A photographic documentary

34. 17 Picturesque Cities on the World Map - A photographic documentary

35. Unforgettable Places from Four Continents, including Trump buildings A photographic documentary

36. Dediu Newsletter, Volume 1, Number 1, 6 December 2016 – Monthly news, review, comments and suggestions for a better and wiser world

37. Dediu Newsletter, Volume 1, Number 2, 6 January 2017 (available also at www.derc.com).

38. Dediu Newsletter, Volume 1, Number 3, 6 February 2017 (available at www.derc.com).

39. London and Greenwich, - A photographic documentary

40. Dediu Newsletter, Volume 1, Number 4, 6 March 2017 (available also at www.derc.com).

Rome: Accademia Nazionale dei Lincei (1603, the oldest worldwide) has its library in Palazzo Corsini (1740), Via della Lungara 10, Roma.

41. Dediu Newsletter, Volume 1, Number 5, 6 April 2017 (available also at www.derc.com).

42. Dediu Newsletter, Volume 1, Number 6, 6 May 2017 (available also at www.derc.com).

43. Dediu Newsletter, Volume 1, Number 7, 6 June 2017 (available also at www.derc.com).

44. London, Oxford and Cambridge, A photographic documentary

45. Dediu Newsletter, Volume 1, Number 8, 6 July 2017 (available also at www.derc.com).

46. Dediu Newsletter, Volume 1, Number 9, 6 August 2017 (available also at www.derc.com).

47. Dediu Newsletter, Volume 1, Number 10, 6 September 2017 (available also at www.derc.com).

48. Three Great Professors: President Woodrow Wilson, Historian German Arciniegas, and Mathematician Gheorghe Vranceanu – A chronological and photographic documentary

49. Dediu Newsletter, Volume 1, Number 11, 6 October 2017 (available also at www.derc.com).

50. Dediu Newsletter, Volume 1, Number 12, 6 November 2017 (available also at www.derc.com).

51. Dediu Newsletter, Volume 2, Number 1 (13), 6 December 2017 (available also at www.derc.com).

52. Two Great Leaders: Augustus and George Washington - A chronological and photographic documentary

53. Dediu Newsletter, Volume 2, Number 2 (14), 6 January 2018 (available also at www.derc.com).

54. Newton, Benjamin Franklin, and Gauss, A chronological and photographic documentary

55. Dediu Newsletter, Volume 2, Number 3 (15), 6 February 2018 (available also at www.derc.com).

56. 2017: World Top Events, But Many Little Known, A chronological and photographic documentary

57. Dediu Newsletter, Volume 2, Number 4 (16), 6 March 2018 (available also at www.derc.com).

58. Vergilius, Horatius, Ovidius, and Shakespeare - A chronological and photographic documentary.

59. Dediu Newsletter, Volume 2, Number 5 (17), 6 April 2018 (available also at www.derc.com).

USA, Boston: a view of the north-east part of Boston, from Cambridge, over Charles River Basin. Federal Reserve Bank Building (187 m, left), and other tall buildings in the financial district.

60. Dediu Newsletter, Volume 2, Number 6 (18), 6 May 2018 (available also at www.derc.com).

61. Vivaldi, Bach, Mozart, and Verdi - A chronological and photographic documentary.

62. Dediu Newsletter, Volume 2, Number 7 (19), 6 June 2018 (available also at www.derc.com).

63. Dediu Newsletter, Volume 2, Number 8 (20), 6 July 2018 (available also at www.derc.com).

64. Dediu Newsletter, Volume 2, Number 9 (21), 6 August 2018 (available also at www.derc.com).

65. World History, a new perspective - A chronological and photographic documentary.

66. World Humor History with over 100 Jokes, a new perspective - A chronological and photographic documentary

67. Dediu Newsletter, Volume 2, Number 10 (22), 6 September 2018 (available also at www.derc.com).

68. Dediu Newsletter, Volume 2, Number 11 (23), 6 October 2018 (available also at www.derc.com).

69. Dediu Newsletter, Volume 2, Number 12 (24), 6 November 2018

70. Da Vinci, Michelangelo, Rembrandt, Rodin - A chronological and photographic documentary

71. Dediu Newsletter, Volume 3, Number 1 (25), 6 December 2018

72. Dediu Newsletter, Volume 3, Number 2 (26), 6 January 2019

73. From Euclid to Edison – revelries in the past 75 years - A chronological and photographic documentary

74. – Socrates to Churchill Aphorisms celebrated after 1960 - A chronological and photographic documentary

75. - Dediu Newsletter, Volume 3, Number 3 (27), 6 February 2019

76. – Hippocrates to Fleming: Medicine History celebrated after 1943 - A chronological and photographic documentary

77. - Dediu Newsletter, Volume 3, Number 4 (28), 6 March 2019

78. - Dediu Newsletter, Volume 3, Number 5 (29), 6 April 2019

79 – Archimedes to Ford: Invention History celebrated after 1943 - A chronological and photographic documentary

80 - Dediu Newsletter, Volume 3, Number 6 (30), 6 May 2019

81 – Sutherland to Pavarotti: Great Singers History - A chronological and photographic documentary

82 - Dediu Newsletter, Volume 3, Number 7 (31), 6 June 2019

A south-west view of Rome from Altare della Patria: Theatrum Marcelli (the Theatre of Marcellus (Marcus Claudius Marcellus, 42 BC – 23 BC, Emperor Augustus' nephew), 13 BC, left back).

Paris (founded circa 250 BC): L'Hôtel National des Invalides (1678), in the 7th arrondissement, with military museums (including details about Lafayette) and monuments, and the burial site for Napoleon Bonaparte, 1769-1821, 52.

100 - Dediu Newsletter, Volume 4, Number 4 (40), 6 March 2020 – World Monthly Report with News and Suggestions for Sustainable Peace, Freedom and Prosperity

101 - Dediu Newsletter, Volume 4, Number 5 (41), 6 April 2020 – World Monthly Report

102 - Dediu Newsletter, Volume 4, Number 6 (42), 6 May 2020 – World Monthly Report

103 – World Constitution Implementation – Moving from violent changes, to smooth transition to the Constitution of the World

104 - Dediu Newsletter, Volume 4, Number 7 (43), 6 June 2020 – World Monthly Report

105 - Dediu Newsletter, Volume 4, Number 8 (44), 6 July 2020 – World Monthly Report

106 - It is getting truer and truer – we urgently need the World Constitution: Moving from anarchic changes, to balanced transition to the Constitution of the World

107 - Dediu Newsletter, Volume 4, Number 9 (45), 6 August 2020 – World Monthly Report

108 - World Constitution with Lovely Comments - Moving from many suboptimal constitutions to the much better Constitution of the World

109 - Dediu Newsletter, Volume 4, Number 10 (46), 6 September 2020 – World Monthly Report

110 – World Constitution with Questions & Answers – Moving from many obsolete constitutions to the much better Constitution of the World

111 - Dediu Newsletter, Volume 4, Number 11 (47), 6 October 2020 – World Monthly Report

112 - World Projects - Moving from minor projects to great projects for the World

113 - Dediu Newsletter, Volume 4, Number 12 (48), 6 November 2020 – World Monthly Report

114 - Dediu Newsletter, Volume 5, Number 1 (49), 6 December 2020 – World Monthly Report

115 - World Opportunities for All - Moving from few local jobs, to world opportunities for all

116 - Dediu Newsletter, Volume 5, Number 2 (50), 6 January 2021 – World Monthly Report

USA, New York: On Broadway at 43rd St, looking southwest, in Times Square

117 - Self-Managing World - Moving from local ruling top-down, to self-managing world

118 – We are all in the same space boat – Peaceful Terra; Moving from local fragile boats to the solid Peaceful Terra

119 - Dediu Newsletter, Volume 5, Number 3 (51), 6 February 2021 – World Monthly Report

120 - All people ask for Peace + Freedom = Prosperity, Moving from local conflicts to world peace and freedom

121 - Dediu Newsletter, Volume 5, Number 4 (52), 6 March 2021 – World Monthly Report

122 - To pour Peace from a cup full of arms, MELT ALL ARMS! - Moving from arms race, to peace enjoyment

123 - Dediu Newsletter Vol 5, Number 5 (53), 6 April 2021 – World Monthly Report

124 - Bureaucracy is growing like a weed - People want a Quality Change; Yup, that's right! Better life for all!

125 - Dediu Newsletter Vol 5, Number 6 (54), 6 May 2021

Italy, Venezia - The south end of La Piazzetta, the south part of Piazza San Marco, with gondole, and wedding pictures of a Japanese couple.

www.ingramcontent.com/pod-product-compliance
Lightning Source LLC
Chambersburg PA
CBHW041309210326
41599CB00003B/41